LONDON TRAVEL GUIDE FOR KIDS

Table of Contents

Introduction — 5

Chapter 1: London 101: Cool Facts and Fascinating History — 6
London: The Fun and Fabulous Basics — 6
   The Language — 7
   The Currency — 7
   The Time Zone — 8
London History: It's Amazing Past — 8
   50 – 300 AD: The Founding of London — 9
   604 – 878 AD: The Building of St. Paul's Cathedral — 9
   1067 – 1176 AD: The Sanction and the Bridge — 10
   1483 AD: King Richard III and the Missing Princes — 11
   1569 AD – The First Lottery — 11
   1600 AD: The Founding of the East India Company — 11
   1897 AD: Queen Victoria's Diamond Jubilee — 12
   1900 AD – Present: The Modern Age — 12

London Traditions: Cool Customs and Fun Festivities   12
   English Breakfast   13
   Sunday Roast   14
   Guy Fawkes Night   14
   Christmas Turkey   15
   RHS Chelsea Flower Show   15
   Trooping of the Colour   15
   Wimbledon   16
   Nothing Hill Carnival   16

Chapter 2: Map and Iconic London Landmarks   17
   Big Ben and the Houses of Parliament   18
   Buckingham Palace and the Changing of the Guard   20
   The Views from The London Eye   22
   The Tower of London and Its History   23
   St. Paul's Cathedral   25
   Covent Garden and Its Street Performers   27
   The Shard   28
   The South Bank   29
   London Bridge   30
   The British Museum   31
   Map of London   33

Chapter 3: Must-See Attractions for Brave Young Explorers   35
   The London Eye   36
   London Bus Tours   37
   Madame Tussauds   38
   The Royal Mews   39

SEA LIFE London   40
Natural History Museum   40
London Dungeon   42
London Zoo   43
Royal Observatory Greenwich   44

Chapter 4: Food Is Where Your Stomach's At!   45
  Beef Wellington   46
  Fish and Chips   47
  Chicken Tikka Masala   48
  Steak and Kidney Pie   48
  Cornish Pasty   49
  Shepherd's Pie   49

Chapter 5: Pre-Trip Fun: Your Adventure Warm Up!   50
  What's in Arthur's Adventuring Backpack?   51
  Arthur's Useful Traveling Tips   55
  Countdown to Fun!   59

Chapter 6: The Adventurer's Journal   60
  How to Journal Your Adventures the Arthur Way   61

Chapter 7: Helpful Resources for Young Adventurers 67
  Helpful Numbers   67
  Handy Apps   67
  Final Words   69

BONUS Coloring Fun: Bring London to Life with Color!   71

Introduction

Well, hello there, and welcome young adventurers to the London Travel Guide For Kids! I'm Arthur (named after the very famous, King Arthur), a Corgi dog adventurer extraordinaire. You may have seen dogs that look like me running around. In England, my breed is very popular because Queen Elizabeth II was a big fan (can you blame her!). Only the best for the Queen, right?
Anyway, I'm here to guide you on your travels through London.

As a Corgi dog, I have been an adventurer my entire life, so I'm more than qualified to show you the ropes! I'm also a London native who knows everything there is to know about this fascinating city. Its history is long, its traditions are interesting, and it has so much to show you.

Your adventures through London may be very different from mine, but all the things you need to know stay the same. Therefore, I'm pleased to take you on a tour of this fabulous city of mine. Without further ado, let's begin! Ruff!

Chapter 1
London 101: Cool Facts And Fascinating History

While you're counting down the days until your adventure, why not read up on some of London's history and get to grips with its many traditions? No, don't start yawning! London's history is super interesting! Trust me, ruff! As an official Adventurers Guild member, old Arthur can explain some of the city's fascinating background and offer some insight into how it all works.

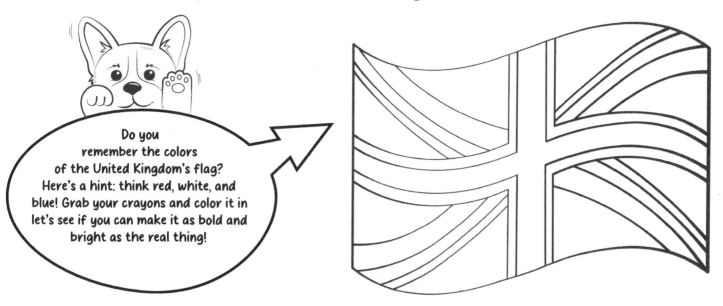

Do you remember the colors of the United Kingdom's flag? Here's a hint: think red, white, and blue! Grab your crayons and color it in let's see if you can make it as bold and bright as the real thing!

London: The Fun and Fabulous Basics

Before we can explore London's interesting history, let's familiarise ourselves with some of the basics. When traveling from another country, there are a few differences to be aware of (like the traffic, for instance), and knowing this information upfront can ensure a smooth adventure.

The Language

London is home to many diverse people from different walks of life. That means that you will probably meet people who speak a different language to you. Which is so cool! However, the main language in London is English (which is the stuff you're reading right now). Even in other parts of the UK – such as Wales and Scotland – English is spoken and understood everywhere you go! There's a few little phrases you should know though. You'll find some people might greet you with, "Alight?" You might think they are asking if you're okay, if something is wrong, but no, that is just their way of saying, "Hi, how are you?"

You could be traipsing around London all day with your new English friend and they might come out with, "I'm knackered!" This means, "I'm so tired!"

The Currency

All the best adventurers will have to deal with money at some point. The currency used in London is the Pound Sterling. The bills feature many famous British leaders, including Winston Churchill and Queen Elizabeth. Take the time to check them out!

The Time Zone

Time is a funny thing. When it's nighttime in one part of the world, it's daytime on the other side of the world. Everything in between is different as well, and these are categorised into different time zones. In London, the time zone works in a strange way if you're not used to it. In fact, there are two time zones: Greenwich Mean Time (GMT) and British Summer Time (BST).

The reason for this is because British clocks are set forward by an hour during summertime. In summer, the days are longer, so people living in London use BST to make better use of the extended daylight!

London History: It's Amazing Past

As we've said before, the key to a successful adventure is preparation, and knowing a place's history is part of the preparation process. A trip is always more interesting when you know a bit about the place beforehand. Don't worry – this is an adventurer's guide, not a history textbook! In this section, Arthur's going to take you through some of the key events in London's long history. 'Prepare' to be surprised at some of London's secret history!

50 - 300 AD - The Founding of London

Okay, so although London is the ultimate British city, you may be surprised to learn that it was not the English who founded it, but the Romans!

Yes! The Romans were the first to build on the land where London sits now. Surprising, right? Ostorius Scapula, the Roman Ruler of Britain at the time, ordered the construction of a fortress on the north bank of the River Thames. That was around 50 AD, which was almost 2,000 years ago!

Later, the fortress was destroyed, and the next version of what we now know as London was built in 290 AD by a different Roman lord. So, you see, we British owe a lot to the Romans!

604 - 878 AD - The Building of St. Paul's Cathedral

A few centuries later, in 604 AD, Mellitus, a priest who travelled with St. Augustine to Britain, constructed St. Ethelbert Cathedral, dedicating it to Paul. As you'll see a little later in this section, people from all kinds of professions didn't let their jobs get in the way of their dreams!

1067 - 1176 AD - The Sanction and the Bridge

In 1067 AD, Emperor William allowed London to exist without Imperial rule. Then, in 1078, Gundulf the Bishop (who may have been a very distant descendant of a certain grey wizard!) founded the London White Tower. Finally, in 1076 AD, work began on a bridge over the Thames.

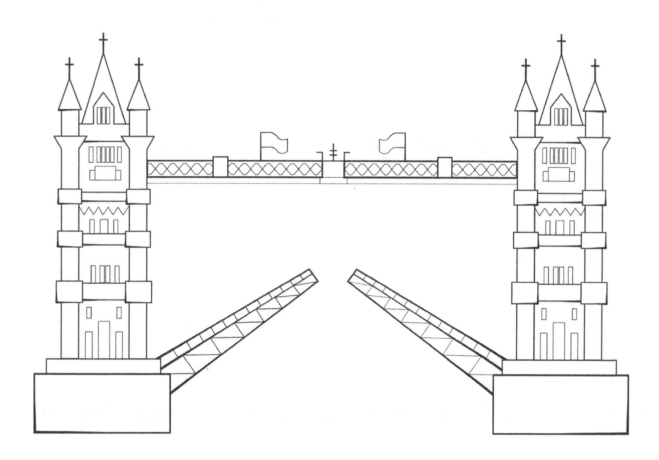

1483 AD - King Richard III and the Missing Princes

Now, here's a real mystery for the young detectives out there. In 1483, Edward V and Richard, the sons of King Henry IV, had a problem. They were supposed to inherit the throne, but their mischievous uncle, Richard III, took over as Regent (which is sort of like a stand-in king!) The new Lord Regent exiled the young princes to the Tower of London and then...

They vanished!
To this day, no one knows what happened to them, where they went, or if they survived. It's a mystery that has intrigued people for centuries and will likely never be solved

1569 AD - The First Lottery

Have you ever entered a lottery? It's funny, we think they've always been around. You see, Queen Elizabeth was facing some financial struggles and the idea came about to raise money through a lottery rather than raise taxes. This money raised was used for things like repairing and strengthening ports and harbors. Prizes included money, tapestries, silverware, land, and other items. The lottery was popular, and well, the rest is history, we still love them!

1600 AD - The Founding of the East India Company

How do you feel about pepper, young adventurer? Well, what if I told you that the price of pepper is ultimately what led to the founding of the East India Company? Sounds crazy, right? But it's true!

Because of the Dutch trading practices that, honestly, go over old Arthur's head, the price of pepper got really expensive, and the British decided that they needed to improve their relations with the East Indies to keep prices down.

And so, the East India Trading Company was born in 1600. The company was probably the biggest corporation in the world! It controlled almost all of the trade between Europe, South Asia, and the Far East. It was so big that it even had its own navy and military!

1897 AD - Queen Victoria's Diamond Jubilee

On the 22nd of June, 1897, Queen Victoria arrived at St. Paul's Cathedral to commemorate – and celebrate – her long 60-year reign.

1900 AD - Present - The Modern Age

Now, London is one of the biggest cities in the world, with a diverse population and a thriving economy. Millions of adventurers like me and you visit it every year because there's so much to see!

London Traditions: Cool Customs and Fun Festivities

Just like any city, London has its very own traditions which make up the city's culture. The keen adventurer should be aware of these occasions and events to truly explore London to its fullest.

English Breakfast

Even new adventurers in London have probably had an English Breakfast at some point. It's a yummy meal that includes beans, bacon, eggs, toast, mushrooms, sausages, and hashbrowns. The meal is so big that you may not even have space for lunch!

Sunday Roast

Another favourite British meal is the good ol, Sunday Roast. This is a meal featuring meat roasted in an oven (usually beef or pork) and served with roasted potatoes, veggies, and a healthy helping of gravy! Oh, my tummy is rumbling just talking about it! It is also typically eaten alongside Yorkshire pudding, which is like pancakes baked in an oven.

Guy Fawkes Night

Every year on the 5th of November, people in London celebrate Guy Fawkes, whose history is a bit of a not-so-once one. However, that's all in the past, really and you can enjoy plenty of fireworks and fun.

Christmas Turkey

In London (and Britain as a whole), it's tradition to eat a turkey after church on Christmas Day. The turkey is normally served with roasted veggies and potatoes, just like a Sunday Roast, but with more crackers and more jokes being shared and more desserts and just more of everything that's good!

RHS Chelsea Flower Show

This beautiful colourful display of flowers has been going on for over 100 years! It sure is a gorgeous sight and worth visiting if you are there at that time of year (May). It's a very popular event, so tell your parents to book tickets early!

Trooping of the Colour

Held at Buckingham Palace, this event is one for those who love all things royal. You'll see hundreds of horses and fancy-looking soldiers. There's music and lots of colour, of course! There's a parade and at the end of it all the Royal Airforce flies over in an exciting display. You may even spot a royal or two!

Wimbledon

If you enjoy tennis, Wimbledon is a lot of fun. This is high-level lawn tennis tournament, and you'll see some famous players. It's in August and you'll notice everything is in white, and don't forget to have the traditional strawberries and cream, so yummy!

Notting Hill Carnival

This has become a major event and it's easy to see why. It's a beautiful celebration of diversity that's been going on for over 50 years now. It's a Caribbean Carnival event with a big parade. You'll see amazing costumes, lots of exciting rides, music bands, stalls, and of course, yummy food.

Chapter 2
Map and Iconic London Landmarks

A city as old as London has secrets around every corner. There's no way for an adventurer even one as skilled as I am to know everything, but I can point you in the right direction!

In this section, old Arthur's going to take you through some of London's most iconic and famous landmarks. Along the way, you will learn about their history. When you put them all together, you should have a pretty good idea of the history of London as well!

Big Ben and the Houses of Parliament

Any young adventurer visiting London for the first time owes it to themselves indeed, to the spirit of adventure itself to visit Big Ben, which is probably the city's most famous landmark. You've probably already heard the tales and seen the pictures, but old Arthur's going to set the record straight.
Big Ben is not a tower it's a bell, and probably the most famous bell in the world at that! The tower that houses it is known as the Elizabeth Tower and reaches

over 100 metres in height! Construction of the tower began in 1843 on the 28th of September, but its famous clock was only started years later on the 31st of May in 1859. The great bell Big Ben himself rang for the first time over a month later on the 11th of July. (Big Ben was Sir Benjamin Hall, Chief Commissioner of Works when the bell was first placed in the tower).

Each of the clock's four faces is nearly 7 metres long, and the minute hands themselves measure 4.2 metres long. That makes the Elizabeth Tower clock the largest four-faced clock in the world!

You're not likely to find something that beats that anytime soon, my young adventurers!

The Houses of Parliament (also known as Westminster Palace) were constructed on the site of a medieval palace that may have been in use since the 11th century. You've got to admit that's pretty cool. The oldest surviving structure is Westminster Hall, which has stood since the reign of King William II, all the way back in 1097! However, construction of the modern version of this grand structure began in 1837 and was completed in 1860, which is pretty old too, come to think of it!

Did you know?

Big Ben isn't the name of the clock or the tower? It's actually the name of the huge bell inside the tower! The tower itself is called the Elizabeth Tower.

Buckingham Palace and the Changing of the Guard

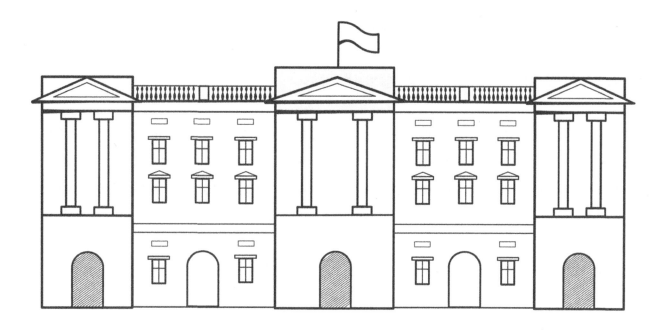

Have you ever wondered where the King sleeps, has breakfast, and goes to the loo? It's easy to forget that he's a normal person, just like you and me, but with a much bigger house!

Buckingham Palace is the King's home in London. It's basically his private hotel, which he stays at whenever he visits London! But Buckingham Palace is much more than that. It is steeped in history and grandeur.

Originally, the palace (then known as Buckingham House) was built for the Duke of Buckingham in 1703. Yes, that's how it got its name, clever ones. It was only acquired by the Royal Family in 1761 by King George III, who gave it to Queen Charlotte for use as her private house. It became the official royal residence in 1837 when Queen Victoria took the throne.

Since then, the palace has gone through a number of changes. It currently contains 775 rooms (!!!): 19 staterooms, 52 royal bedrooms, 78 bathrooms, 92 offices, 188 staff bedrooms, and around 300 other rooms!

The palace is also the site of the traditional Changing of the Guard, an annual display of British tradition that is viewed by millions all over the world. The ceremony involves the swearing-in of new guards to patrol the palace grounds. Yes, those funny fuzzy tall hats are actually made of bearskin! Who knew? Well, I did!

Of course, my own ancestor had a palace just like this once, but probably not as big. I think it was called Camelot, or something like that...

The Views from The London Eye

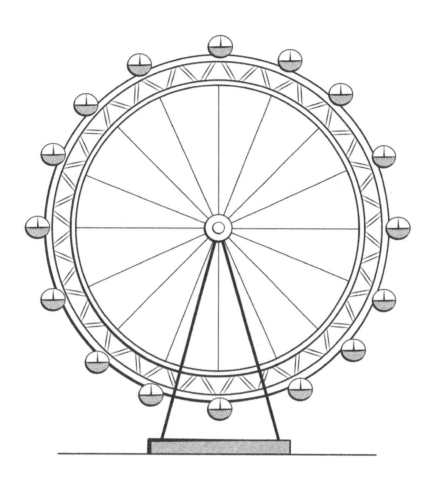

As a new young London adventurer, you may think that all the best things to see in London were built at least a hundred years ago. In fact, the city has many modern marvels, and the most famous of these is the London Eye.

The London Eye (also known as the Millennium Wheel) was built in 1999, just before the turn of the millennium. It was the world's tallest Ferris wheel for seven years until it was surpassed in 2006 by the Star of Nanchang. Don't worry, it's still huge!

The London Eye actually reaches over 135 metres in height and is one of the city's most popular attractions, visited by millions every year. From its peak, you can easily catch a full view of this amazing city and even spot some of the sights you've visited. The wheel was fitted with LED lighting to make it even more visible and beautiful at night.

The London Eye is so popular, that it sparked renewed interest in Ferris wheel construction all around the world.

The Tower of London and Its History

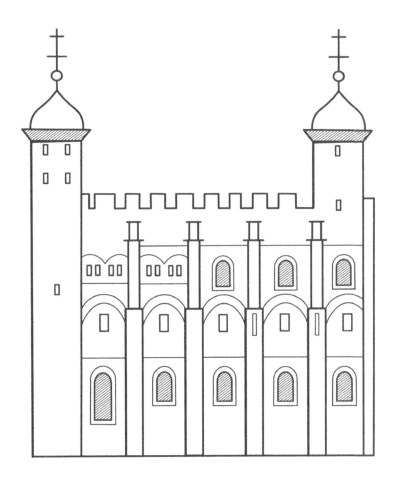

Young adventurers may already be familiar with Big Ben, Buckingham Palace, and the London Eye by sight alone. After all, these three structures are probably stand out the most in the whole city. But there's another historic building that any good young adventurer should visit.

Yes, the Tower of London can be thought of as the original seat of power in the city, long before Buckingham Palace. It was built in 1066 by William the Conqueror as a symbol of Norman power. It was cleverly positioned on the River Thames to act as both a fortress and a gateway into the capital.

Although the tower has undergone many renovations over the centuries, its basic structure remains, making it one of the longest-standing medieval structures in the world! It is visited every year by tourists and adventurers like your young selves from all over the world and is still an iconic symbol of British influence. It really is amazing that is it still standing after all that time.

Still, it's nothing like Camelot, from what I've heard....

Did you know?

Ravens have lived at the Tower of London for centuries! According to legend, if they ever leave, the kingdom will fall. To keep the legend alive, there are usually at least six ravens living there, cared for by special Ravenmasters to make sure they never all fly away!

St. Paul's Cathedral

Cathedrals are exciting places to visit for eager young adventurers! Although they have a religious significance, they also stand on their own as architectural marvels, containing great beauty and ingenious design!

While the Tower of London has mostly stood strong since its construction all the way back in 1066, St Paul's Cathedral has had a much more tricky history. The current structure can be considered the fifth version of the cathedral. The original building occupied a site that was previously used as a Roman temple. The first

Christian cathedral was built in 604 AD, but it was burned to the ground. The second cathedral (built at the same site) was destroyed by Viking raiders, and the third cathedral (built in 1087) also burned. What bad luck with cathedrals, hey?

Finally, the fourth cathedral (known as Old St. Paul's) was constructed in the late 11th century and was one of the biggest buildings in Europe at the time! Its spire was taller than the current building's dome, but it was struck by lightning in 1561 and was never repaired. Eventually, the cathedral fell into disrepair once more. Oh, bad luck strikes again!

Finally, after a massive setback caused by a fire, a man named Christopher Wren designed new plans for the cathedral in the 1660s. His plans were only approved the following decade, in 1675, when work began in earnest and continued until 1710.

Since then, the cathedral has gone through some changes to its look but has otherwise stood its ground. Let's hope no more lightning strikes occur in the area!

Did you know?

St. Paul's Cathedral has a special spot called the Whispering Gallery. You can whisper against its walls, and someone on the opposite side can hear you!

Covent Garden and Its Street Performers

Forgive old Arthur for rambling I'm a big fan of history, ruff ruff! You see, I grew up on the tales of my ancestors, of King Arthur and his knights, and although no one can prove he existed, between you and me, I'm fairly certain he did!

That being said, I understand that not every young adventurer wants to be a student of history! So, instead of rambling on about some old building, why don't I tell you about a more modern institution that you can visit right now?

Simply put, Covent Garden is the place where young travelers like you can get their shop on! It's a huge, sprawling market home to many shops, theatres, restaurants, and pubs (for your adventurous parents only)! There is a lot to do here you can visit the Royal Opera House, the London Transport Museum, Somerset House, and of course, the famous Covent Garden Market, where you can find almost anything you can think of!

For London newbies, there is almost no better place in all of London to truly roam around and explore in a safe and secure environment!

Did you know?

Covent Garden is like a playground for performers! You can find amazing street artists there doing magic tricks, juggling, and singing. It's always fun to stop and watch a show while exploring the market! Who knows? You might even see a new talent every time you visit!

The Shard

So far, the London Eye has been the most recent London construction, but there's another exciting London structure that young adventurers should visit when they get the chance!

The Shard is the tallest building in London, measuring 309 metres in height that's 72 stories! The Shard is so big that you can see it from almost anywhere you stand in London. While not yet as iconic as Big Ben, it is an important British landmark.

Construction of the Shard began in March 2009. Its development was led by an Italian architect named Renzo Piano. Mr. Piano wanted to design a building whose construction differed from that of other modern skyscrapers and he sure achieved that!

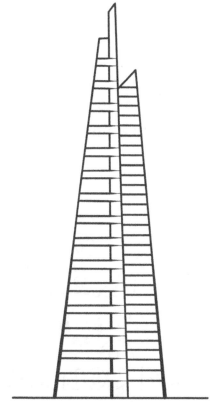

The Shard was built from the top down. That means that the building's core was built even as the foundations were still being dug. The Prime Minister, John Prescott, only approved of the building because he thought the design was exceptional and he was right!

True to its name, the Shard is like a great big spike, rising up to the sky from the very heart of London. Some people were initially upset by its image when it was finally completed in 2012, (you can't please everyone!) but it has since become a magnificent symbol of London and British culture as a whole.

The South Bank

Don't go anywhere yet old Arthur's still got one more fantastic London landmark that young adventurers should visit during their stay in this great city.

The South Bank Centre is named because it is located on the south bank of the River Thames. It is a popular destination for tourists (like you!) and locals alike. Here, you can find three main performance venues: Royal Festival Hall, Queen Elizabeth Hall, and Purcell Room.

The first performance venue was the Royal Festival Hall, which was completed in 1951 and was the main location for the Festival of Britain. From 1962 to 1965, work was completed to extend the building, and a few years later, Queen Elizabeth Hall and Purcell Room were open to the public.

Today, the South Bank Centre hosts a variety of performances, including 2000 paid performances and 2,000 free performances. A lot, right?! There are also a variety of educational programmes that are hosted here, so keen adventurers would do well to pay the South Bank Centre a visit. Tell your folks!

Did you know?

There's a hidden river under the streets of London? The River Fleet flows beneath the city and joins the River Thames near Blackfriars Bridge.

London Bridge

London is full of interesting landmarks there are so many that it would be impossible to account for all of them in one section of this book alone!

London Bridge is one such iconic structure. You've probably heard its name in that old nursery rhyme! "London Bridge is falling down, falling down, falling down London Bridge is falling down, my, fair, lady!" You know the song? You don't? Well, if not I suggest you look it up, it's super famous. However, that song actually refers to the old London Bridge and not the one that was built in its place.

That bridge was actually built by the Romans all the way back in 43 AD. Yes, those Romans again! Since then, it has been built upon and extended, and has stood for 2000 years. Unbelievable. It also marks the spot of the most ancient crossing of the River Thames.

Now, here's a fun fact: many people often confuse London Bridge with Tower Bridge! While London Bridge is a simple, straightforward bridge that connects the City of London to Southwark, Tower Bridge is the one with two big towers and a unique drawbridge that opens to let tall boats pass. Tower Bridge is often considered the more famous of the two because of its impressive design! You can check it out in this illustration!

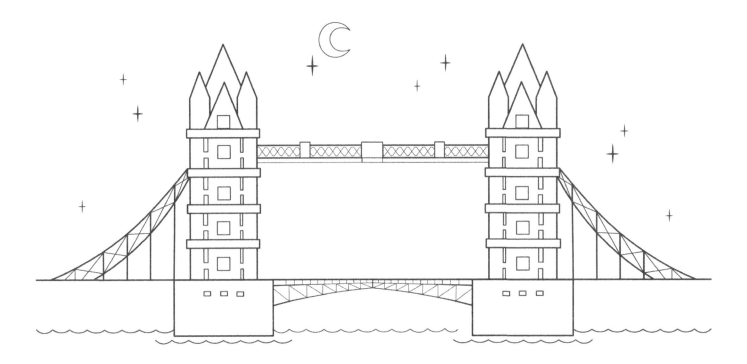

And London Bridge is still used today! It just goes to show how much of London is still steeped in ancient history a history that you can explore during your adventures through this wonderful city of ours.

The British Museum

Alright, alright Arthur's got one more famous British landmark for you! This one should be particularly interesting for adventurers.

The British Museum is actually the oldest public national museum in the world. It first opened in 1759 and welcomed travellers from all over the world. Its subjects, all the interesting things stored inside it, are wide and varied and it's the perfect place for curious adventurers to visit if they're looking to broaden their knowledge.

Look 👀
Rosetta Stone
Elgin Marbles
Oxus treasure

Some of the museum's most famous artifacts include the Rosetta Stone, the Oxus Treasure, and the Elgin Marbles, all of which are recognised all over the world for their importance and significance to human history.

The British Museum is also responsible for the opening of the Natural History Museum, which old Arthur will tell you about in a bit.

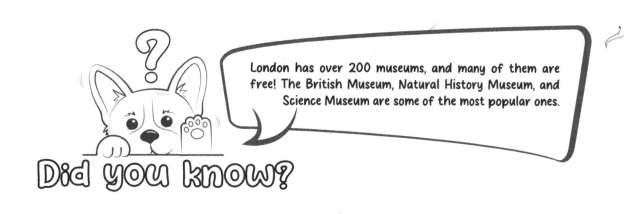

Did you know?

London has over 200 museums, and many of them are free! The British Museum, Natural History Museum, and Science Museum are some of the most popular ones.

Chapter 3

Must-See Attractions for Brave Young Explorers

Eager young adventurers will want to see everything there is to see in London, but the truth is that the city has so much to offer that you probably won't see it all during your first adventure. Luckily, old Arthur always comes prepared. Here is the Unofficial Adventurers Guild List of Attractions for Young Adventurers:

The London Eye

You may think old Arthur's going a little crazy yes, this is the second time I've mentioned it in this book already! Don't worry; I've still got all my wits about me.

It's just that it needs repeating because this should be on any young adventurer's travel itinerary! The London Eye is Europe's tallest Ferris wheel, and I just need to make sure you don't miss it!

Naturally, its popularity almost guarantees that you will be waiting in line for some time before finally getting to ride it! But it's worth it! You won't find a more beautiful view of London anywhere else in the city (except maybe the Shard), and it is especially magical at sunset when the sun casts pink and orange light across the River Thames.

Let old Arthur fill you in on a secret: you can skip the queue with a fast-track ticket! They are very expensive so you will need to ask your adventuring parents if it's in the budget. With a fast-track ticket, you can reach the end of a three-hour queue in two minutes! Don't tell anyone what I told you, though.

Did you know?

The London Eye is the world's largest cantilevered observation wheel. It's as tall as 64 red double-decker buses stacked on top of each other!

London Bus Tours

Another iconic London symbol is the double-decker bus! It's an exciting way to get around the city, especially for new and visiting adventurers like yourselves.

There are many bus tours available in London, and they are designed specifically for adventuring families like your own! The tours will take you all over the city, visiting every famous landmark on the way (including many of the ones old Arthur's already mentioned). You will get great explanations for every historic site, which, when combined, will give you the full story of this great city. So easy!

However, I know that you young adventurers can get ants in your pants after a while! Luckily, the tours are not too long, meaning you'll still have plenty of time for more adventures in the city.

The famous red double-decker buses weren't always red. In the early 1900s, different bus companies used different colors to stand out. Red became the standard color in 1907.

Madame Tussauds

Imagine all your favourite heroes coming to life. How exciting is that? If only there was a place built for this exact purpose...

Wait a minute there is! Madame Tussauds is an exciting place to visit in London. It houses life-size wax figures of famous figures all around the world! That includes actors, members of the Royal Family, and even football stars. Remember that football is very popular in London don't make the mistake of calling it soccer!

Madame Tussauds also hosts many fun events that allow young adventurers like you to interact directly with all your heroes. Unfortunately, my petition to be included has been unsuccessful when you visit, do let them know about old Arthur, won't you?

The Royal Mews

Unfortunately, Buckingham Palace is closed throughout most of the year. Not even old Arthur can get in there! Luckily, the Royal Mews is a great way to get acquainted with the royal side of London.

The Royal Mews is a very peaceful location and a nice break from the hustle and bustle of London. There is not much to do here except look around and gasp at the beautiful carriages that are on display! Be on the lookout for the Gold State Coach, which is drawn by a whopping eight horses. Oh, and you should also look at the Diamond Jubilee State coach. Oh, and the Glass Coach, which has been used extensively by the Royal Family since the 18th century. These coaches really are the stuff of fairytales.

Visiting the Royal Mews doesn't take long, meaning you will have plenty of time for other adventures, but it is a great way to slow down a little and catch a glance at the life of royalty!

SEA LIFE London

For those young adventurers who just can't get enough of the London Eye, here is another excuse to pay it a visit. SEA LIFE London is located right next to the famous Ferris wheel. It's an aquarium filled with interesting exhibits, fun games, and, of course, some wonderful animals, including sharks!

Honestly, old Arthur is a bit too scared to visit here, but brave adventurers like you would have a great time exploring the aquarium! The whole trip only takes an hour and a half, so you will have plenty of time to get around and see more of lovely London.

Natural History Museum

If you're an adventurer, then the chances are you're also a keen student of history! After all, an adventure is a collection of exciting stories, and all the places you visit will have stories of their own to share.

The Natural History Museum is the place to go if you want to learn more about the world we live in. It is one of three museums in the area, the other two being the Victor and Albert Museum and the Science Museum.

The Natural History Museum is home to over 80 million different items! These specimens come from all over the world, from different periods of time. In fact, some of the items contained within the museum were collected by none other than Charles Darwin himself, a famous scientist and philosopher.

But that's not all. Don't you think a good adventure needs a terrifying monster to confront? Well, the Natural History Museum is home to many huge dinosaur skeletons. One of its ceilings also features a giant blue whale skeleton!

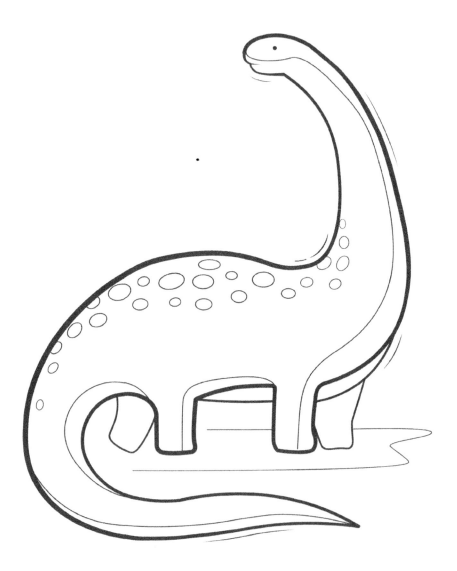

The museum is also home to a very big library containing many books, journals, and manuscripts that have been collected over the years. The library can't be visited whenever you want (you'll need to make an appointment), but the museum itself is free to enter so there's nothing stopping you from this exciting part of your adventure!

London Dungeon

If you're an older adventurer, you may be on the lookout for some excitement more suitable to your age group. Warning: This is not for adventurers under the age of 12!

The London Dungeon is the definition of scary! Well, I'm a bit of a scaredy cat, I mean, dog, but many seem to love it. It's a tourist attraction famous for its spooky atmosphere, but as any adventurer knows, adventuring is brave work.

The dungeon can be found in London's South Bank. It was opened in 1974 and recreates some bizarre, spooky, and scary moments in British history with actors, props, and special effects with a healthy dose of humour as well!

Be warned, however: the London Dungeon is not for the faint of heart! I think I mentioned that, eeek!

London Zoo

The last attraction on our list is the London Zoo. Any adventurer, no matter their age, has a fondness for animals, and the zoo is the best place to see them!

The London Zoo is the world's oldest scientific zoo, opened in 1828. At first, it was only used for scientific and research purposes, but more animals were brought to live there, and pretty soon, it became a popular place for animal lovers to visit!

Today, the zoo is home to more than 14,000 individual animals and is visited by millions of people every year it's one of the largest zoos in Europe!

Royal Observatory Greenwich

Alright, alright I promise this will be the last one that old Arthur tells you about today. Don't worry, it's an interesting one!

The Royal Observatory is the oldest surviving scientific institution in Britain. It was founded by King Charles II in 1675 (in Greenwich, of course). Its sole purpose was to observe the skies the "heavens" and record the movements of the stars, planets, and other astronomical bodies.

More so than that, however, the Royal Observatory is also the spot which marks the Prime Meridian, longitude 0'0'0'. This line is responsible for splitting the western and eastern hemispheres of the world and it's also where we get Greenwich Mean Time, the standard measurement of time in Britain and many other parts of the world!

Today, the Royal Observatory still stands as an iconic British landmark and is visited by Brits and people from all over the world who come to see the famous longitudinal divide.

Chapter 4
Food Is Where Your Stomach's At!

All that adventuring you're going to be doing will eventually wear you out! When that happens, the best cure is a nap and a steaming, warm plate of food!

Luckily, the British have a bunch of fun, delicious meals for you to try. These can be found all over London and are a must for any young adventurer to try before the end of their quest.

Beef Wellington

When you're craving something scrumptious and meaty, you can't go wrong with some Beef Wellington. This is a dish primarily made from steak, which is then rolled up into a delicious, crunchy pastry. It's popular all throughout the UK, and you can find it in many restaurants in London.

Fish and Chips

If you had to ask the next Londoner you meet what their favourite dish is, the chances are that they're going to answer with fish and chips. This meal is a cornerstone of British culture, so any young adventurer exploring London should try it out. You can find it almost anywhere you look. Crispy, fried fish, crunchy fried chips, a little vinegar to sprinkle over, and wrapped up in newspaper is sometimes how it's done! My suggestion is, if you have time, to head to the seaside — they taste even better, trust me!

Chicken Tikka Masala

For those young adventurers keen to taste some more exotic flavours, you can't go wrong with chicken tikka masala! Although it has its roots in Asian cuisine, this is a favourite dish of many British people and, indeed, many people in London as well! And if you're feeling a little chilly, this will warm you right up.

Did you know? London is one of the most diverse cities in the world, with food from all over the globe. You can find everything from traditional British fish and chips to delicious Indian curry!

Steak and Kidney Pie

In general, you can expect to come across many different pies throughout your adventures in London. British people sure do love their pies, and steak and kidney pies rank among the most popular! This is a dish best served in a restaurant and can quickly fill you up to prepare you for your next adventure.

Cornish Pasty

Pastry is an important element of British cuisine. It's a comfort food for many, and it doesn't get more cozy, warm and tasty than a Cornish pasty. These small pasties are packed with both meat and vegetables and are a great healthy snack to eat while continuing your adventure. They can be found in bakeries all over London.

Shepherd's Pie

Shepherd's Pie is a classic British meal that originated in the North of England and Scotland. It's made from minced lamb and potatoes, though some people use beef instead, which actually makes it a cottage pie! This one may be difficult to find as it's usually eaten at home, but savvy adventurers will be on the lookout for it whenever they step into a new restaurant! Or, better still, make some London friends and hope they invite you home for dinner and make you a Shepherd's Pie!

Chapter 5
Pre-Trip Fun: Your Adventure Warm Up!

A trip to London is an exciting adventure, but as any good young explorer knows, the key to a successful adventure is preparation. Don't worry – you won't be expected to do any homework! Preparing for your trip can be a fun little task in and of itself, and it's a great way to get excited in the lead-up to your adventure!

"Well, that's all well and good," I hear you say, "but what on earth am I supposed to bring, Arthur?"

Don't you worry! Arthur's got you covered.

In this section, I'll tell you what to pack for your trip to London – all the essentials like umbrellas, a toothbrush, you name it. I'll also tell you what you can expect when you arrive in London and give you a look at some useful tips and tricks that old Arthur's picked up over the years.

Now, let's get on with the prep…

What's in Arthur's Adventuring Backpack?

Let's kick things off with some packing essentials. A good adventurer needs good adventuring equipment, after all.

Warm Clothes

Now, you've probably already heard about what the weather is like in London. While you may experience a few days of sunshine during your adventure, you will probably experience just as many cold and gloomy days as well, if not more. It gets chilly!

Take Arthur's advice: pack warm clothes, or clothes that are easy to layer-up. If you're not sure of what to wear, take a look at the official Adventurers Guild list of the best clothes to pack for a trip to London:

- A cozy comfy beanie
- A warm jumper or two (or three!)
- Some woolly socks
- A raincoat
- A pair of warm gloves

Think about how long you'll be staying in London. It's a good idea to pack several of these items so that you don't have to walk around London in the same outfit every day! You should also pack a few summer clothes, just in case the weather clears up. T-shirts under jumpers work well, you can throw your jumper off and tie it around your waist when the sun peeks out, then easily throw it back on when it cools again. That's the kind of scene you can expect.

"But Arthur, what about shoes?"

How could I forget? You'll need some good shoes as well to go along with your socks and keep your feet warm.

London is easily explored on foot, so be sure that the shoes you bring are comfy sore feet can quickly spoil your adventure!

It can get pretty rainy too, some wellies (you might call them gumboots!) are great for keeping feet dry!

Toiletries

Now, now, don't zip that bag up yet there are a few more essentials we need to pack before we can get started on our adventure.

Think about all the little, everyday things you use at home you'll need them for your trip to London as well! Luckily, the official Adventurers Guild List of Essentials for the Budding Adventurer can point you in the right direction if you're having trouble. Here's the basics:

- Trusty toothbrush (and some toothpaste!)
- Useful dental floss
- Deodorant or body-spray
- Moisturiser
- Make-up
- Mini shampoo and conditioner
- Mini shower gel or soap

If you take any medication, you'll want to make sure that you pack it as well. I would also suggest that you bring some sunblock along if you are going on your adventure during the summer. For winter adventures, pack some chapstick to keep your lips moisturised the winter air can quickly dry your lips.

Gadgets and Electronics

The modern adventurer almost always comes equipped with a smartphone or tablet. Hopefully, you'll only need these to take pictures and stay in contact with your fellow adventurers there's plenty to see in London without your digital devices!

Don't worry, old Arthur knows how important these gadgets are, which is why I've secured this list for you young adventurers: the Official Adventurers Guild List of Essential Gadgetry for Young Adventurers:

- Chargers for all of your devices
- A 220v 3-pin to 110v adapter
- A good pair of earphones
- A laptop bag
- An external power pack

You may also want to bring a camera along to take pictures during your adventure. If you do, make sure that you keep it safe in its bag, and bring along an extra memory card in case you run out of space for all those pictures!

Miscellaneous

Now, there are a few other items that you will need to consider. These don't fall under any of the previous categories, so the Adventurers Guild has released the Official List of Miscellaneous Items for Budding Adventurers:

- Your passport
- An umbrella
- Physical copies of documentation (ask your parents about this one!)
- Book or magazine
- Jewellery hairbands
- Sunglasses
- Swimwear
- Hat

And, of course, you'll need your trusty journal to write down all your quests and record your adventures in London. I'd also suggest you bring along a map to get an idea of your surroundings and where you're going!

Once you've packed everything, you're just about ready to start your adventure. But don't go anywhere yet Arthur's got some useful tips to help young adventurers get started.

Arthur's Useful Traveling Tips

In this section, I'll go over some handy tips that will make your adventure even better and help you get around easier. The Adventurer's Guild hasn't made the list official, so for now, let's call it Arthur's Unofficial Handbook of Tips and Tricks for Young Adventurers:

Be Mindful of Traffic

You may be travelling from a country where the traffic drives on the right. Here in London, traffic drives on the left stick to the pedestrian crossings and don't leave your fellow adventurers' sight!

Keep Your Umbrella Handy

Your umbrella is your best friend in London the weather here can be rather temperamental, so you can expect plenty of rain or at least some drizzle. Keep your umbrella with you at all times the rain can come at any moment!

Don't Take the Tube Everywhere

London is famous for its underground subway network. It's an easy and convenient way to get from one side of the city to the other. However, you may find walking to be easier, more interesting (and quicker) in some situations. Consult your map to find out whether you need to take the tube or if walking might be a better option!

Shop On Weekdays

London is home to some pretty cool and unique shops, but they tend to get crowded pretty quickly, especially on the weekend. Set aside a day or two during the week to visit some of the shops with your fellow adventurers!

Get it Right, and Stand On the Right of an Escalator

The people of London are always on the move, headed this way and that. Some people are always in a hurry, so always stick to the right when riding an escalator to let others pass you on the left.

Explore With a Local

You and your fellow adventurers may be super excited to see everything London has to offer, but it's easy to get lost. Consider joining a tour to get the full London experience without losing your way.

Countdown to Fun!

Now that you're fully prepared for your adventure, all that's left to do is wait for it to begin. Sometimes that's the hardest part! But you're in luck because you can count down the days until your trip with this: the Official Adventurers Guild Countdown Calendar:

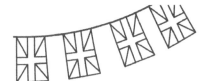 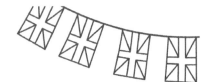

London

HERE I COME!

35	34	33	32	31	30	29
28	27	26	25	24	23	22
21	20	19	18	17	16	15
14	13	12	11	10	9	8
7	6	5	4	3	2	1

DAYS TO LONDON

Chapter 6
The Adventurer's Journal

All good adventurers keep a journal with them at all times. This allows them to keep track of all their quests and adventurers the places they've been, the places they'll go and what they think of it all!

Indeed, my young adventurers, it's important to set aside some time to reflect on your journey! Exploring is only half the fun, you see the things you learn along the way make the adventure worth it.

For this section, there are a few things you will need:

- A blank notebook or journal
- Some colourful pens and pencils
- Some pictures of your adventure
- Postcards, tickets
- Stickers
- Stamps

How to Journal Your Adventures the Arthur Way!

Unfortunately, while the Adventurers Guild is a respected, resourceful institution, there are no official courses on how to journal for young adventurers. Luckily, I'm around to give you some guidance on how best to reflect on your journey.

Step 1: Start with a Prompt

For some young adventurers, writing can be a bit of a challenge. The important thing to remember is that there is no wrong way to write! This isn't school where you will be marked and graded on your grammar, spelling, and handwriting – this is an adventure, and that means excitement!

I always start with a prompt. It's a general idea that gets my old brain working! When you're just starting out with your journal, your prompt may be something like "The First Place I Visited" or "What I Saw Today." It can be anything, though! The main goal is to keep a record of your thoughts and feelings throughout your adventure and those things are unique to you alone.

If you're in a pinch, however, old Arthur's collected some great prompts over the years to get you journaling in earnest!

- Describe the interesting things or souvenirs you bought during your adventure
- Describe the different people you met during your adventure
- Describe the yummy foods you ate during your adventure
- What was a funny thing you saw or heard?
- What's the best place you visited?
- What is the best day of your adventure?

You may come up with other prompts and ideas as you write. Keep these in mind for later! There is never a bad time to write.

Step 2: Make It Colourful

All young adventurers will have their own way of writing things down. Try to think of your journal as a book of memories when you remember something, you remember the pictures, not the words!

In this case, it can be great fun to add some colour to your journal, making certain ideas pop out from the rest. For this, you can use coloured pens, pencils, highlighters, crayons, markers, and pastels anything and everything you can think of! You can even add stickers you've picked up on your travels.

It's a good idea to give each heading or prompt in your journal a different colour. This will help them stand out from the others. You can also collect pictures from your adventure cut out some magazines and newspapers to give your adventure journal even more personality! Don't forget tickets from the places you've visited.

Step 3: Add Some Pictures

For this step, I hope you brought your camera along or smartphone! While you may not be able to develop or print any of the photos you've taken on your adventure just yet, keep them safe for later! You can spruce up your journal with pictures of your adventure keep an eye out for pretty sights and memorable moments. London is full of them!

Extra Journal Prompts

For this step, I hope you brought your camera along or smartphone! While you may not be able to develop or print any of the photos you've taken on your adventure just yet, keep them safe for later! You can spruce up your journal with pictures of your adventure keep an eye out for pretty sights and memorable moments. London is full of them!

In case you're running out of ideas for what to include in your next journal entry, old Arthur's got some more prompts for you to pick and choose.

- What was the best part of your day, and what was the worst?

- What is something new you learned during your adventure?

- Quote something funny someone said. (People in London have great senses of humour)

- What did your toys or stuffed animals think of your adventure?

- Interview someone you're adventuring with.

- Make up a pretend postcard to be delivered to one of your toys back home.

- Review a restaurant or attraction you visited.

- Create a pretend advertisement for one of the places you visited during your adventure do your best to sell it!

- Draw a map of your adventure and include all the best places.

- Write down interesting phrases you've heard.

- Come up with your own "How To" guide for something you did during your adventure.

- Describe the different animals you met.

- Draw your favourite adventuring outfit.

- Write down some adventuring tips of your own old Arthur won't mind!

- Design a book cover to reflect your adventure.

- List 5 facts you learned about one of the places you visited.

- Design a T-shirt for one of your favourite places.

- Make a list of cool souvenirs to bring home with you.

- Describe the best day of your adventure.

- Log the weather!

- List some of the best and worst smells you encountered during your adventure.

- Come up with a soundtrack for your adventure.

Remember, there's no wrong way to journal, but if you're ever stuck, you know old Arthur's got your back!

Chapter 7
Helpful Resources for Young Adventurers

Remember what old Arthur said way back at the beginning of this guide the key to a successful adventure is preparation. When you're adventuring through a new place, you will need to ensure your safety and the safety of the people you're travelling with! I'm sure you're not adventuring alone!

Your travel companions should already come equipped with a few helpful resources for getting around London. If you're in doubt, have a look at the Official Adventurers Guild Guide to Helpful Resources in London.

Helpful Numbers

- City of London Information Center (+44 20 7332 1456) (perfect for tourists to find information, directions, and even suggestions on ways to spend a day out).
- 999 or 112 for emergency call centres.
- Victoria Visitors Center (+44 343 222 1234) (helpful for ticket advice, maps, souvenirs, and finding the best attractions).

Handy Apps

- Trainline (sells tickets and railway cards and provides information on train schedules and live times for trains all throughout Europe).
- Wise (International currency transfer app).
- National Trust (information on natural and historical information on a particular location).
- Get You Guide (easy access to local tickets and tours).

Final Words

And that's all old Arthur's got for you today! Hopefully, you're all set to embark on what will surely be one of the grandest adventures in your life! The City of London is brimming with stuff to see and things to do. Throughout this guide, you should have learned about:

- All the essential things to pack
- Useful tips and tricks to kickstart your adventure
- A brief history of London
- Famous London traditions and fun events
- The most iconic landmarks and buildings in London
- The must-see attractions to visit during your adventure
- How to journal during your adventure
- How to collect your memories into a single book
- Handy numbers and resources to use

Of course, there is so much more to learn, but those things come with time and experience. Take it from me I've been adventuring my whole life. And I'm a dog, so everything takes even longer for me! The best thing you can do is explore, experience, and create.

Oh, and before you go don't forget to have fun with the coloring pages! Grab your crayons, markers, or whatever you like best, and make those London scenes as colorful as your imagination. After all, the adventure doesn't stop just because you close the book!

So, what are you waiting for, young adventurer? There's a whole city waiting for you to explore, and after that, the rest of the world, too. Who knows maybe we'll see each other again. Ruff, ruff!

BONUS Coloring Fun:
Bring London to Life with Color!

77

Made in the USA
Middletown, DE
26 January 2025

70283447R00046